P9-DER-161

The Usborne Book of
Really Awful
Jokes

Designed and illustrated by Leonard Le Rolland

Edited by Laura Howell

Additional research by Alastair Smith

Managing designer: Ruth Russell

Americanization editor: Carrie Seay

CONTENTS

School Daze

Our class is like a zoo!

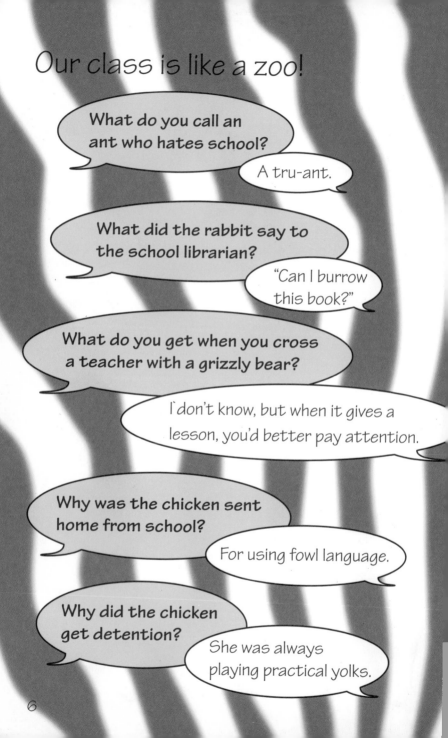

What *do* you call an ant who hates school?

A tru-ant.

What did the rabbit say to the school librarian?

"Can I burrow this book?"

What *do* you get when you cross a teacher with a grizzly bear?

I don't know, but when it gives a lesson, you'd better pay attention.

Why was the chicken sent home from school?

For using fowl language.

Why *did* the chicken get detention?

She was always playing practical yolks.

I'm sick (of school)

Nurse, I can't stop clucking, and it frightens me.

Oh, don't be such a chicken.

Nurse, I'm in the school band and I swallowed my harmonica. What should I do?

Be thankful you don't play the piano.

Nurse, I think I've turned into a cookie.

Yes, you do look a bit crumby.

Nurse, I've got lettuce sticking out of my ear.

Oh dear. I fear that it may be just the tip of the iceberg.

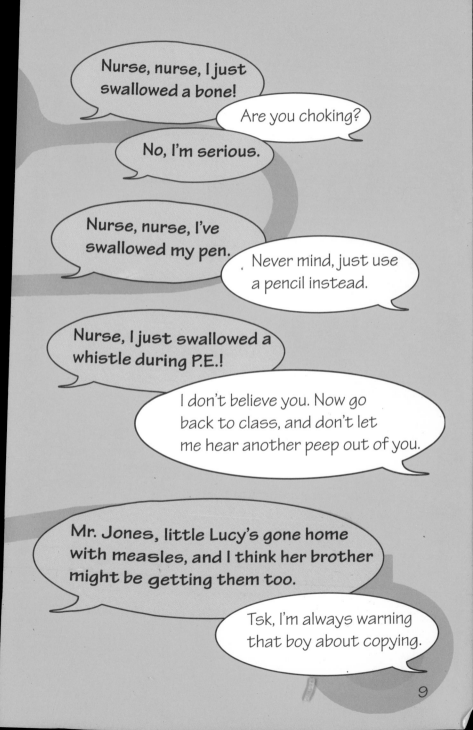

9

I'm still sick!

Nurse: Billy, you're always coming to see me. What's wrong with you this time?

Billy: I sprained my ankle running down the hall.

Nurse: That's a lame excuse.

Kid: Nurse, I feel like I'm turning into a pancake.

Nurse: Oh, how waffle.

Kid: I had trouble with diarrhea at school today.

Mother: That's terrible! I didn't know you were ill.

Kid: I wasn't, I just couldn't spell it.

Kid: Nurse, I keep thinking I'm the school bell.

Nurse: Take these tablets, and if they don't help, give me a ring in the morning.

Kid: Nurse, are you absolutely sure this cream will cure my terrible acne?

Nurse: Of course, I never make rash promises.

Kid: Nurse, I keep thinking I'm a headlouse.

Nurse: I wish you'd get out of my hair.

Kid: Nurse, I just can't stop stealing from the other kids.

Nurse: Hmm, have you taken anything for it?

Kid: Nurse, the other kids tease me. They say I smell like a fish.

Nurse: You poor sole.

Why did the class joker go to the hospital?

To learn some sick jokes.

Nurse: How did you get that black eye?

Kid: You see that tree outside?

Nurse: Yes...

Kid: Well, I didn't.

Career day

Kid: I want to be a policeman and climb trees all day, like my dad.

Career advisor: Policemen don't climb trees, dear.

Kid: My dad does, he told me he works for the special branch.

Career advisor: Do you have a career in mind?

Kid: I think I'd make a good book keeper.

Career advisor: Why's that?

Kid: Well, I've had some library books since my first day at school.

Career advisor: Tell me, what would you like to be when you grow up?

Kid: I want to be a lumberjack.

Career advisor: Hmm, do you really think you can hack it?

Kid: Do you think I'd make a good plumber?

Career advisor: Maybe, but you might find the work too draining.

Kid: When I leave school, I'd like to be a baker. I hear they make lots of dough.

Career advisor: Well, you're certainly good at loafing around.

Career advisor: What does your dad do for a living, Bobby?

Bobby: He sits around and makes faces all day.

Career advisor: How unusual. Is he some kind of entertainer?

Bobby: No, he works in a clock factory.

Career advisor: I see. And what does your mother do?

Bobby: She shoots people and blows them up.

Career advisor: Don't be silly!

Bobby: It's true, she's a photographer.

14

www (world wide wackiness)

Kid: Sorry I'm late. I dreamed I was surfing the Web.

Teacher: How could that make you late for school?

Kid: I had to go back to sleep to switch off the computer.

How does the class joker send messages?

By tee-hee mail.

Kid: I went to this Web site to find out what a citrus fruit is, but it won't work.

Teacher: Hmm, perhaps the lime is busy.

Who has the best Web site in the animal world?

The Onlion King.

Teacher: I'm a bit worried about letting you repair my expensive new laptop.

Computer teacher: Don't worry, of all the computers I've ever repaired, only one has ever blown up.

Teacher: How many computers have you repaired?

Computer teacher: This will be my second.

Mandy: What should you do if you get lots of e-mails saying "What's up, Doc? What's up, Doc?"
Andy: Check for bugs in your system.

Peter: I use the Internet to tell me what the weather's like.
Anita: How do you do that?
Peter: I carry my laptop outside and if it gets wet, I know it's raining.

Kid: Would you mind e-mailing my test results to my parents?
Teacher: But your parents don't have a computer.
Kid: Exactly!

Why were the kids in computer class scratching their heads?
They had internits.

School Library

Birdwatching — Jack Daw

Diary of a Bank Robber — HANS UPP

WHEN DOES SCHOOL END? — WENDY BELLGOES

SPORTS DAY — Willy Win, illustrated by **Betty Wont**

Healthy Breakfast Foods — Lena Bacon

Adding for Beginners — Juan & Juan Mextoo

Getting into Trouble — Kermit Crimes

A Week Off School — Trudi Light

HELP WITH YOUR HOMEWORK — Linda Hand

Finding a Penpal — Miles Apart

THE **BIG** BANG — Dinah Mite

The Story of the Titanic — Mandy Lifeboats

Tree Felling — Tim Burr

Noise in the Classroom — Constance Snoring

Never Give Up

Bullying is Wrong — Howard U. LyKit

Strong Winds — Gail Force

Coping with Grief — Anne Guish

Looking at Insects — Amos Keeto

How to Succeed — Vic Tree

The Effects of Storms — Rufus Blownoff

School: the Early Years — L.M.Entree

Eating Garlic — Y. I. Malone

The Arctic Ocean — I. C. Waters

Coping with Exams — Gladys Over

THE WORLD'S BIGGEST ANIMALS — Hugh Mungus

Learning to Share — Ken I. Havsum

The World's Biggest Problem — Major Setback

Th Bi P

Play Music — Roland Rock

Learn to Behave — Bea A. Goodchild

Art Class

A spider doing push-ups on a mirror

The Eiffel Tower (at night)

A pea on a skateboard

A squirrel climbing a tree

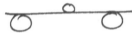

Aunt Joan weeding in the garden

A chameleon hiding on a melon

A seagull flying upside down

An ant with bad breath

Two eggs climbing a pyramid

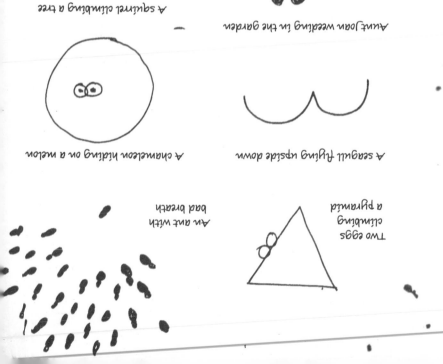

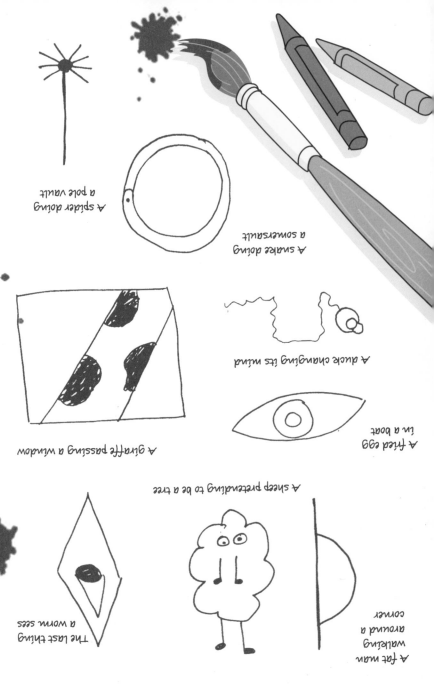

A spider doing
a pole vault

A snake doing
a somersault

A duck changing its mind

A giraffe passing a window

A fried egg
in a boat

A sheep pretending to be a tree

The last thing
a worm sees

A fat man
walking
around a
corner

21

Food, glorious food

Mother: Why have you been sent home from school early?

Kid: I set fire to something in cooking class.

Mother: That's a bit careless. What was it?

Kid: School.

Drew: Can you tell me what's in this cake you made?

Lou: Why, are you going to try making one?

Drew: No, my doctor might need to know.

Cooking teacher: Jenny, what are the best things to put in a fruit cake?

Jenny: Your teeth.

Jane: My cooking teacher didn't like what I made in class today.

Wayne: What did you make? A pie? A pizza?

Jane: A big mess.

What do the parents of the richest kid in school make for dinner every night?

Reservations.

Peter: I always know when dinner's ready in our house.

Rita: Why, do your parents call you?

Peter: No, the smoke alarm goes off.

Barry: How do you think they keep flies out of the school cafeteria?

Gary: Maybe they let them taste the food.

Teacher: Stop this food fight at once! Do you have any idea what goes into preparing your school meals?

Kid: Yes, that's why we started throwing them instead of eating them.

Teacher: What started that food fight in the cafeteria?

Kid: The bread rolls, Mr. Lee. Next came the cheese pie, and finally dessert.

It's a
dirty job...

**Teacher: Why are you wearing
two jackets?**

Janitor: Because I'm about to paint the hallway and it
says on the can that two coats are best.

**Janitor: Can I play on the school soccer team
next season?**

Soccer coach: Yes, I think you'd make a
good sweeper.

**Teacher 1: Do you find the new janitor a
little unfriendly?**

Teacher 2: Yes, I tried talking to him the other day and
he gave me the brush-off.

**Teacher: My goodness, you sound terrible.
You really should take something for that cold.**

Janitor: Good idea. I'll take the rest of the week off!

What *do* you call a pair of janitors?

Partners in grime.

Janitor: I quit!

Teacher: Why? What's the matter?

Janitor: Nothing really, it's just time I made a clean sweep of things.

Did you hear? Miss White ran off with the janitor.

Really?

Yeah, I heard he swept her off her feet.

I once had a classmate named Britt,
Who thought that he was quite a wit.
When I disagreed,
He said "Well, you need
A funnybone transplant, you twit!"

Joke school

Ever wondered how comedians learn to be funny? They go to Joke School, where making your teacher laugh is the only rule!

Teacher: OK class, can anybody tell me what is yellow, has big teeth and lives in a fruit bowl?
Pupil: Sorry, no idea.
Teacher: A banana. I lied about the teeth.

Teacher: What's the definition of a snail?
Pupil: It's a little slimy animal with a hard shell.
Teacher: Wrong, wrong, wrong! It's a slug wearing a crash helmet.

Teacher: Why do doctors' bags snore?
Pupil: But that's silly. They don't snore, they're bags!
Teacher: Yes they do... because they're full of sleeping pills.

Teacher: Can anyone give me a definition of politics?

Pupil: It's the name given to the complex relationships between those in power and the people they govern.

Teacher: Wrong! It's what happens to your pet parrot if he swallows a clock.

Teacher: Class, do you know why tall people have long arms?

Pupil: Because if they were short they'd be out of proportion with the rest of their bodies?

Teacher: Nonsense! It's because if their arms were shorter they wouldn't reach their hands.

Teacher: What's green and scaly and goes "Hith, hith"?

Pupil: I give up.

Teacher: It's a snake with a lisp, of course!

Teacher: What's a clamera?

Pupil: Don't you mean camera?

Teacher: No, a clamera is what you get if you cross a shellfish with a picture-taking device.

Teacher: What goes moo, baa, oink, woof, quack?

Pupil: I don't know.

Teacher: Come on, at least try to be funny. It's a cow that can speak five languages.

Teacher: Why do elephants have wrinkled feet?

Pupil: Er, because their shoes are too tight?

Teacher: Correct! Now you're getting the hang of things.

Teacher: What did the baboon say when it swallowed a stick of dynamite?

Pupil: Ba-boom!

Teacher: Yes! You are an excellent student.

Teacher: How do you know if there's an elephant in your refrigerator?

Pupil: Ooh, I think I know this one – your nose touches the ceiling?

Teacher: Good try, but wrong punchline. The answer is, you find footprints in the butter.

Teacher: How do you keep a skunk from smelling?

Pupil: Remove his scent glands.

Teacher: Wrong! You hold his nose.

Teacher: What did the bird say when it laid a square egg?

Pupil: There's no such thing as a square egg, is there?

Teacher: You are a terrible student! The answer is simply "Ouch!"

Teacher: What kind of bus crossed the ocean?

Pupil: A bus is a land vehicle. It couldn't cross the...

Teacher: No, no, no! The answer is Colum-bus!

Teacher: What kind of key opens a banana?

Pupil: That's a trick question. You don't need a key to open a banana.

Teacher: Wrong. The answer is a monkey.

Teacher: You, boy. What kind of lights do you think Noah used on his ark?

Smart kid: I believe oil lamps were commonly used in that era, sir.

Teacher: That may be correct, but it doesn't make me laugh. He used floodlights.

Teacher: What is the hardest thing to eat?

Pupil: Er, a rock cake?

Teacher: No, a banana.

Pupil: Bananas aren't hard to eat...

Teacher: Clearly you've never tried to eat one sideways.

Teacher: Tell me, what do you call a pig with three eyes?

Pupil: Some kind of horrible mutant?

Teacher: Not at all. It's a piiig.

Teacher: Does anyone know what is orange and sounds like a parrot?

Pupil: Erm, some kind of canary or bird of paradise?

Teacher: Not even close. The answer is a carrot.

Teacher: How does one recognize a dogwood tree?

Pupil: By its small size and attractive white blossoms.

Teacher: Probably true, but not very amusing. The answer is, you listen to its bark.

Teacher: What do we know about a bird in the hand, class?

Pupil: That it's worth two in the bush?

Teacher: Well, I'd say it makes it hard to blow your nose.

Teacher: Why is a pea small and green?

Pupil: Because it contains chlorophyll.

Teacher: No, because if it were big and yellow, you might mistake it for the school bus.

Teacher: How do you fit an elephant into a matchbox?

Pupil: Erm, I don't know.

Teacher: Take out the matches, obviously! Now let's try that again. How do you fit a hippo into a matchbox?

Pupil: Take out the matches?

Teacher: No, take out the elephant!

Teacher: Why do hummingbirds hum?

Pupil: It's the noise their wings make as they beat them

Teacher: Don't be ridiculous. It's because they don't know the words.

Teacher: Tell me, if frozen tea is iced tea, what is frozen ink?

Pupil: Iced ink.

Teacher: Well, take a bath then!

Teacher: What kind of animal has four legs and can see just as well at both ends?

Pupil: Surely some kind of mythical beast?

Teacher: Really? What about a horse with its eyes closed?

Teacher: Why do you think a stork lifts one leg?

Pupil: Some kind of evolutionary quirk?

Teacher: Don't try to be too clever. If it lifted both legs, it would fall over.

Can anyone answer this: when is a car not a car?

When it's become scrap metal?

Not bad, but the answer is when it turns into a side street.

Teacher: Today's lesson is about riddles. What flies but never goes anywhere?

Pupil: Um... a lost homing pigeon?

Teacher: Good try, but the answer is a flag.

Teacher: What is a kitten after it's fourteen days old?

Pupil: A young cat?

Teacher: No, no. It's fifteen days old.

Teacher: What has fifty legs, but can't walk?

Pupil: Let me think... half a centipede?

Teacher: Not bad, but the answer is twelve and a half tables.

Teacher: What kind of room can you never enter?

Pupil: I'd say a room without a door.

Teacher: Good guess, but no. It's a mushroom.

Teacher: Tell me, boy. What is red and invisible?

Pupil: I don't know, I can't see it.

Teacher: Try harder. The answer is no tomatoes.

Teacher: Can you name something that is full of holes, yet can still hold water?

Pupil: But if something has holes, the water would leak out.

Teacher: Haven't you ever seen a sponge?

Teacher: What goes "Oom, Oom"?

Pupil: Some kind of siren?

Teacher: Ridiculous! It's a cow walking backwards.

Teacher: Tell me, what do you think would happen if you threw a blue stone in the Red Sea?

Pupil: Well, red and blue make purple. So would it turn purple?

Teacher: Of course not. It would just get wet.

Teacher: What pet do you think makes the loudest noise?

Pupil: Hmm... perhaps a parrot or a big dog?

Teacher: Think more carefully. It's a trumpet.

Teacher: What is black and white and red all over?

Pupil: A penguin with sunburn!

Teacher: Well done! I also would have accepted an embarrassed panda or a nun with a nosebleed.

Teacher: What would happen if you were to cross a dog with a plant?

Smart kid: I'm sure modern genetic technology wouldn't allow such a thing.

Teacher: What? Haven't you ever seen a field full of collieflowers?

Teacher: Class, what has four legs and flies?

Pupil: I've heard this one. It's two pairs of jeans.

Teacher: Don't be silly. It's a dead cow.

Teacher: Think carefully. What is green and square?

Pupil: Let's see... a football field? A pool table?

Teacher: Wrong. It's an orange in disguise.

Teacher: What's the difference between a piano, a fish and a tube of glue?

Pupil: Don't know.

Teacher: You can tune a piano, but you can't tuna fish. Get it?

Pupil: But what about the glue?

Teacher: Ah, I thought that's where you'd get stuck.

I must say, you're the most well-behaved and academically-minded pupils I've taught in a long time.

Thank you, teacher!

I'm very disappointed in you all. Stay behind after school and write "I must fool around more in class" on the board one million times.

But – !

Only joking.

The Great Outdoors

Further afield

The school went on a field trip to the Natural History Museum in London. "How was it?" asked Jimmy's mother when he returned.

"It was the worst zoo I've ever been to," he replied. "All the animals were dead!"

Pupil: Mr. Smith, what's big and red, and has ten legs and fangs?

Teacher: I've no idea, why do you ask?

Pupil: Because one just crawled up your pants leg.

Mother: Did you enjoy the field trip today, dear?

Kid: Oh yes. In fact, we're going back tomorrow.

Mother: Really, why?

Kid: To try and find the kids we left behind.

Teacher: I'm thinking of taking my class to the zoo tomorrow.

Principal: Certainly not! If the zoo wants them, they can come and collect them.

Teacher: Tom, we carry whistles on a hike in case of an emergency. Don't blow yours all the time.

Tom: But I'm using it to scare away tigers, Mr. Lee.

Teacher: There are no tigers here.

Tom: That proves how well the whistle works.

Teacher 1: Why do you dread taking your pupils overseas?

Teacher 2: Because every time they get on a ferry, it makes them cross.

Wendy: That cow over there is a pretty shade of brown, Miss White.

Teacher: Yes, Wendy. It's a Jersey.

Wendy: Really? I didn't know cows wore jerseys...

Fun and games

Soccer coach: Why didn't you stop the ball?

Kid: That's what the net's for, isn't it?

Sunita: My brother wanted to enter a marathon, but he decided to go to college first.

Rita: Why was that?

Sunita: Our parents always told us that education pays off in the long run.

Kid: Coach, the soccer field's flooded. What should we do?

Coach: Bring on the subs.

Teacher: Jane, write out "I must not forget my P.E. bag" 100 times.

Jane: But Mr. Jenkins, I only forgot it once.

Barry: What's the difference between the school soccer team's goalkeeper and Cinderella?

Carrie: Cinderella got to the ball.

Why are you swimming on your back?

You told us never to swim on a full stomach.

Joan: Why are the kids from art class no good in sports matches?

Jane: They keep drawing.

Katie: Why don't you play football with Martin any more?

Kevin: Would you play with someone who cheats and kicks people all the time?

Katie: No...

Kevin: Well, neither would he.

Teacher: Who was the fastest runner in history?

Kid: Adam, because he came first in the human race.

Johnny: I can't believe I just missed that goal. I could kick myself.

Jimmy: Don't bother, you'd probably miss.

Billy: My P.E. teacher wouldn't listen to me when I said I was no good at throwing the javelin.

Lily: What happened?

Billy: Oh, he got the point eventually.

P.E. teacher: Hey! Don't dive into that swimming pool, there's no water in it!

Kid: It's OK, I can't swim.

Benny: What has eleven heads and runs around screaming?

Lenny: The school hockey team.

P.E. teacher: It is a well-known fact that exercise kills germs.

Kid: But how do you get the germs to exercise?

P.E. teacher: Why won't you attempt the high jump?

Kid: I'm scared of heights.

P.E. teacher: Well, try the long jump then.

Kid: I can't do that, I'm short-sighted.

Kid: I don't think I made the school shot putt team.

Dad: Why not?

Kid: The coach said I was so bad, I couldn't throw myself to the floor.

Molly: Who's the best-looking boy in school?

Holly: The leader of the running team, because he's always dashing.

Meanwhile, on the playground...

Ricky: I'm having a bad day, all my teachers are criticizing me.

Lucy: Really?

Ricky: Yeah, in fact, my art teacher just said I'm so talentless, I couldn't draw breath.

Karen: It's true there's a link between television and bad language.

Darren: How do you know?

Karen: I told my teacher I'd watched TV instead of doing my homework, and she yelled at me.

Gary: Do you want to walk back home through the spooky graveyard tonight?

Barry: No way, I wouldn't be seen dead there.

Are you trying to make a fool out of me?

No, I never like to interfere with nature.

Andy: My **teacher's a peach.**

Mandy: You mean she's sweet?

Andy: No, I mean she has a **heart of stone.**

What do you call a teacher with chalk in his ears?

Anything you like, he can't hear you.

What do you think you're doing, telling everyone I'm stupid?

Sorry, I didn't know it was supposed to be a secret.

Jez: **What kind of car does your dad have?**

Les: I can't remember, but I think it starts with t.

Jez: **Really? My dad's starts with gas.**

What's the difference between an ice cream cone and the meanest kid in school?

You lick one, the other licks you.

You two boys! Stop fighting at once. You should learn to give and take.

We did. He took my sandwich and I gave him a slap.

Gina: The toughest kid in school threatened to hit me if I didn't give him my lunch.

Sabrina: That's awful!

Gina: You don't know my mother's cooking. He offered to do my homework if I took it back.

Big kid: I'm gonna mop the floor with your face, kid.

Little kid: Hah, you'll be sorry.

Big kid: Oh yeah, why's that?

Little kid: You won't be able to get into the corners very well.

Teacher: If you had ten chocolates, and the boy next to you took away seven, what would you have?

Kid: A big fight, Mr. Lee.

Teacher: Why are you crying, Sophie?

Sophie: Anna broke my new ruler.

Teacher: How did she do that?

Sophie: I hit her with it.

Teacher: Who broke this window?

Carl: It was Lenny, Miss Smith.
I threw an apple at him and he moved away.

You've been fighting again, haven't you? Look, you've lost your two front teeth.

No I haven't, Mr. Lee. They're in my pocket.

A teacher whose temper was short,
Would shout, when a pupil was caught
With no homework to show,
"To the corner you'll go,
Where you'll stay 'til you do
as you're taught!"

Test stress

I hope I didn't see you looking at Anna's test paper.

I hope you didn't see me, too.

I don't think I deserve zero for this test, Mr. Lee.

Nor do I, but it's the lowest grade I'm allowed to give you.

I'm taking tests in French, Spanish and algebra this year.

If you're so clever, let's hear you say "Hello" in Algebra.

Why shouldn't you put gel on your hair the day before a test?

If you did, all the answers might slip your mind.

Les: Great news, teacher says we'll have a test today come rain or shine.

Jez: What's so great about that?

Les: It's snowing outside!

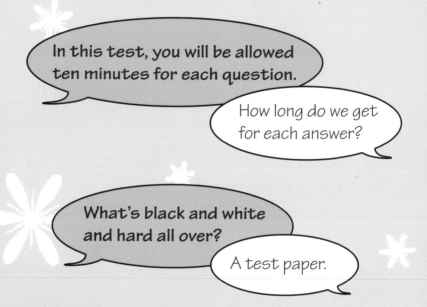

In this test, you will be allowed ten minutes for each question.

How long do we get for each answer?

What's black and white and hard all over?

A test paper.

Why did the skeleton schoolgirl stay late at school?

She was boning up for her tests.

Dad: Were your test results good?

Kid: Yes and no.

Dad: What do you mean, "yes and no"?

Kid: Yes, my test results were no good.

Dad: Why did you get such a low score in that test?

Kid: Absence.

Dad: You were absent on the day of the test?

Kid: No, but the boy who sits next to me was.

How did you do in your tests?

I failed everything except history.

How did you manage that?

I didn't take history.

What do you get if you cross a vampire and a teacher?

Lots of blood tests.

Mother: How were the test questions?

Kid: Easy.

Mother: Why do you look so miserable, then?

Kid: The questions didn't give me any trouble, but the answers were really hard.

General knowledge

1. What important discovery led Archimedes to leap out of his bathtub and shout "Eureka!"?

That the water was too hot.

2. Where are the largest animals found?

In the sea because they won't fit anywhere else.

3. Name a bird of prey.

The priest's pet canary.

4. If a person from Rome is called a Roman, what is a person from Paris called?

A parasite.

··

History

5. What did Napoleon become on his 30th birthday?

A year older.

6. Where was America's Declaration of Independence signed?

At the bottom.

English

7. What is the most important thing to remember about grammar?

Shes a bit deaf so you need to speak loudly to her.

8. What should you do with double negatives?

Don't never use them.

....

Physics

9. Describe the process of conduction.

The way the sound of music spreads from one place to another

Chemistry

10. Name a type of hard water.

Ice

11. Describe the periodic table.

An item of furniture that you don't use all the time.

Human biology

12. What does a blood vessel do?

Carries Count Dracula across
the sea.

13. Explain the process of respiration.

When you breathe you inspire. When
you don't you expire.

14. What is a skeleton?

A person with his insides out and
his outsides off.

15. What is the fibula?

A small lie.

16. When might you have an ultrasound test?

When you buy a new CD player.

17. How are genes inherited?

When my brother grows out of them.

Earth and space

18. Describe the equator.

It is an imaginary lion running all around the Earth through Africa.

19. Give a fact about the Sun.

Some people use the Sun to tell the time but I've never been able to see the numbers.

20. Name two things you might find on the seabed.

Sea sheets and sea pillows.

....

Science

21. Describe a magnet.

A little white thing that you might find in a rotten apple.

22. Define momentum.

Something you buy to remind yourself of a place you visited.

Ghoul School

Ghostly goings-on

What do little ghosts do their homework in?

Exorcise books.

What position did the ghost play on the school soccer team?

Ghoulkeeper.

What did the ghost teacher tell her pupils?

"Spook when you're spooken to!"

What do ghosts play in the school band?

Haunting melodies.

How do they learn to play them?

They study the sheet music.

Ghost kid: My hamster ate my homework.

Ghost teacher: Don't try your lame excuses on me. I can see right through you.

Did you hear about the ghosts who went to the school dance?

They had a wail of a time.

Where do ghosts get an education?

High sghoul.

I'm having a funny spell...

What is a little witch's best subject in school?
Spell-ing.

**How did the little witch know
when it was time to go to school?**
She looked at her witchwatch.

**Why was the teacher confused when he had
to teach a pair of witch twins?**
He couldn't tell which witch was which.

What did it say on the witch's report card?
Her work is good, but there's broom for improvement.

Why did the witch teachers go on strike?
They wanted sweeping reforms.

How do you know if you're sitting next to a witch in class?
She has a big "W" on her pencilcase.

Kid 1: Are you having a birthday party this year?
Kid 2: No, I'm having a witch do.
Kid 1: What's a witch do?
Kid 2: She flies around on a broomstick, of course.

What was the name of the little witch's father?
He was cauld-ron.

67

Rib-tickling skeleton jokes

What instrument did the little skeleton play in the school band?

The trom-bone.

What do you call a skeleton who's late for school every morning?

Lazy bones.

Why didn't you go to the school dance?

I had no body to go with.

What happened when the ghost teachers went on strike?

They were replaced by a skeleton staff.

Sghoul dinner menu

Starters

Tomb-ato soup
Dread rolls

Main courses

Spookghetti
Monster mash with grave-y
Ghoul-ash
Devilled eggs
Baked beings
Fried lice
Toads in the hole

Desserts

Ice scream
Booberry pie
Blood oranges
Leeches and cream

There was a young werewolf named Mary,
Whose body was terribly hairy.
Her classmates would scoff,
"If you shaved it all off,
we'd still think you're ugly and scary!"

Simply monstrous

Why are little monsters so good at adding?
They can count up to 25 on their fingers.

What's the difference between a nice teacher and the Loch Ness Monster?
There's a chance the Loch Ness Monster might exist.

How do monsters like their eggs served in the school cafeteria?
Terror-fried.

What game do monsters like best?

Swallow my leader.

Why was the monster teacher getting angry?

Everything he told his class went in one ear and out the others.

Why was the two-headed monster bad at geography?

Because he never knew if he was coming or going.

Teacher: What would you do if you saw a huge, green monster?

Kid: Hope it hadn't seen me first.

Why did the one-eyed monster give up teaching?

He only had one pupil.

Did you hear about the monster teachers who got married?

It was love at first fright.

Why did the yeti go to the school nurse?

He was feeling abominable.

How does Quasimodo bring his sandwiches to school?

In the lunch pack of Notre Dame.

Why did the school cook shout at the troll?

She saw him goblin his food.

Kid: Dad, the other kids are mean to me. They call me a werewolf.

Dad: Be quiet and comb your face.

Why did the little werewolf get asked so many questions in class?

Because she always gave snappy answers.

Did you hear about the cannibal
who was expelled from school?

He was buttering up his teacher.

How do you spot a cannibal
kid in the school cafeteria?

He asks for the cook.

Why was Frankenstein's
monster best friends with
the class joker?

She always kept him in stitches.

Why did the two cyclops
children fight?

They couldn't see eye to eye
over anything.

Vampires

What happened to the vampires on sports day?

They finished the race neck and neck.

What do vampires learn in school?

The alpha-bat.

Did you hear about the vampire who was in the school play?

He had a bit part.

What do polite vampire children say?

Fang you very much.

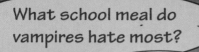

What school meal do vampires hate most?

Stake and fries.

Why did the little vampire go to the school nurse?

He was always coffin.

What after-school club do vampire children join?

A blood group.

Why did the little vampire join art class?

He was good at drawing blood.

77

Die laughing

Why did the little vampire have no friends in school?

Because he was a pain in the neck.

What was the little vampire's idea of fast food?

Someone with high blood pressure.

What did the little vampire have with his apple pie in the school cafeteria?

Vein-illa ice cream.

Teacher, I studied really hard. Did I pass my test?

I'm sorry, Vlad. All your efforts were in vein.

Why do demons and ghouls sit together in class?

Because demons are a ghoul's best friend.

Why was the zombie school so popular?

Kids were dying to get into it.

Why do zombies study Latin and Ancient Greek?

Because they like dead languages.

Who did the zombie take to the junior prom?

Any old girl he could dig up.

My literature teacher, Miss Mann,

Wrote poems that never would scan.

When asked "Why's that so?"

She said "I don't know,

But maybe it's because I always try to

cram as many words into the last line

as I possibly can!"

Dikshunry

The book that helps you write
"right" or "write" right

A

Abundance A dance which is held in a bakery.

Accidents Emergency teeth to temporarily replace those knocked out by mistake.

Acorn Something painful on my dad's toe.

Acrobat Kind of flying creature that shows off a lot.

Adverse A poem that seems to get longer the more you read it.

Afford Popular type of car.

Antelope Event involving two bugs who fall in love and run away together.

Apex A gorilla's old girlfriend.

Arrest Something you take when you are tired.

Atom Male cat.

Automate Robot's best friend.

B

Baleful A word which describes a barn filled with hay.

Barbarian A hairdresser called Ian.

Battery A place where you keep small, winged mammals.

Beehive An order given by bees to their misbehaving children.

Belly dancer A ballet dancer, spelled badly.

Berets What French people put in fruit pies.

Blazer A jacket that is on fire.

Blood brother Dracula's closest relative.

Bombastic A long, thin explosive, like dynamite.

Bulldozer A male cow, asleep.

Butterfly Genetic experiment involving a bird and a goat.

C

Cabbage A taxi's age.

Camelot A herd of north African humped animals.

Carnation A country where everyone owns a car.

Carpet A dog that sits in its owner's vehicle all day.

Castanets What Spanish fishermen do when they go fishing.

Chili powder Very fine snowflakes.

Chinchilla Special device for cooling the lower jaw.

Circumference The knight who invented the round table.

Cocktail Drink made from a rooster's rear end.

Commentator A talking spud.

D

Dark Ages Knight time!

Deadline Perimeter of a cemetery.

Decide You'll find this just around from defront.

Denial Big river in Egypt.

Disband When members of a rock group fall out with one another.

Dogmatic Kind of robot dog.

Dogma A puppy's mother.

Doing The noise a spring makes.

Donation A country full of female deer.

Dramatic That terrible business you have to go through to get that wretched parasite off your dog's back.

tic

Barney

E

Earwig False hair that comes down over the ears.

Eclipse What a male gardener does to a hedge.

Elastic band An old rock group that keeps bouncing back.

Elderberry Wisest fruit on the branch.

Electric eel Fish that thrives in strong currents.

Electroplate What atomic scientists eat their dinner from.

Emulate What people do when they copy the movements of a very large Australian bird.

Encumber The watery bit in the middle of a cucumber.

Exhale Like frozen rain, except that it's now turned slushy.

Explosion Result of experiment.

F

Fan belt What a soccer fan uses to keep pants up.

Father-in-law Dad, in jail.

Fiction What a teacher thinks of your homework excuses.

Fiddlesticks Violin bows.

Fillet What you say to a gas station attendant.

Finale Good quality French beer.

Fiord Norwegian car.

Flamenco A big, pink, dancing bird.

Flattery A worn-out electricity source.

Flea market Where dogs go to get their next infestation.

Flippant A small, industrious bug on its back.

Flypaper What spiders decorate their homes with.

G

Gaggle The sound a group of geese make when you tell them a joke.

Galleon A unit of measurement used on very old ships.

Gangrene To be feeling sick.

Gastronome An elf-like creature with indigestion.

Genius A very intelligent person who lives in a magic lamp.

Geranium A nuclear fuel that smells nice.

Gigantic The biggest, scariest bug in your dog's fur.

Glossary Paint store.

Goblet A genetically modified, small turkey.

Grammar Grandad's wife.

Granivore A monster that devours grandmothers.

H

Halo A word that angels use to greet each other.

Hamlet Small piece of pork.

Handicap Useful headgear.

Hasty A quick, delicious snack.

Hatchet What a hen does to its egg.

Hogwash Pig's laundry.

Holy What my old socks are.

Honesty A fear of being caught.

Honeycomb Hair styling tool used by bees.

Hornet What a goat does with its head to something that it doesn't like.

Housefly A small insect with wings, six legs and a roof.

Humbug Musical insect.

85

I

Ice cream What I do when scared.

Idolize Lazy eyeballs.

Ignoramus A big, stupid animal that wallows in mud.

Illegal Bird of prey with ailment.

Impeccable Hidden from birds.

Independent Something, e.g. a picture, enclosed in a locket worn around the neck.

Infamy To feel persecuted, e.g. "They've all got it infamy!"

Information How planes fly at an air show.

Inkling A very small pen.

Intense Where you sleep while camping.

Isopod Hi-tech igloo.

J

Jailbait Prison food.

Jape You little monkey!

Jargon Fancy word for the loss of a glass receptacle.

Jeans What chromosomes wear.

Je ne sais quoi Sorry, I don't know what this means...

Jitterbug Insect that's had too much coffee.

Joan of Arc Noah's wife.

Joint account Money saved up to buy meat.

Jubilant Triumphant insect.

Juggernaut Jug full of nothing.

Jumbo Flying elephant.

Justice What's left in the glass after you've drunk the lemonade.

Juvenile Small African river before it got huge.

K

Karate A drink enjoyed by martial artists.

Keratin What preserved carrots are sold in.

Ketchup Command shouted at tomato that is slowest to ripen.

Kettle drum What musicians boil water in.

Khaki What soldiers use to make their vehicles start.

Kidnap Something that a young child takes when tired.

Kidney That thing halfway down a kid's leg.

Kindred Fear of being visited by relatives.

Kinetics Science of understanding your family.

Kinship The family's boat.

Kit fox A self-assembly mammal.

L

Landmark Imprint made by unsuccessful skydiver.

Lassitude A heroic dog with attitude.

Launch Midday meal for astronauts.

Launch pad To throw a notebook at a classmate.

Lavish Resembling a lavatory.

Lazy bones An idle person's skeleton.

Legend The foot.

Light sleeper Someone who falls asleep with the light on.

Locomotive A crazy reason for doing something.

Logarithms Tunes played at a lumberjack's birthday party.

Lyre A very dishonest musical instrument.

M

Macro Scottish bird.

Malady The correct way to address a female aristocrat.

Mammoth Giant flying bug thing.

Marigold To become the wife or husband of somebody who is very, very rich.

Maritime Wedding day at the seaside.

Market What teachers do to homework.

Melancholy Dog that likes watery fruit.

Milk shake Drink given by nervous cows.

Mothball What moths play football with.

Mug What a thief drinks from.

Mutant Genetically altered ant.

N

Naturalist Carefully compiled information about plants and animals.

Newfangled Grandpa shows off his latest set of dentures.

Nightingale To spend a night outside in the wind.

Night school Academy where Dracula and the wolfman went to study.

Nipper Baby crab.

Nitty-gritty How a dirty scalp looks, up close.

Noble gas What a lord fills his car with.

Noisette Small, crunching sound a nut makes when it is cracked.

Norm Just a regular kinda guy.

Novelty Unusual-tasting herbal beverage.

O

Observant What a biology teacher tells you to do when out looking for bugs.

Occidental Something unplanned that happened in the Far East.

Octopus Strange, genetically modified, eight-legged cat.

Offal Something dreadful.

Offense Aggressive-looking boundary around your house.

Operatics Bugs that live in an opera house.

Operetta Person who gives tuneful advice if you have trouble using your phone.

Opportune Music played by entertainer on a pogo stick.

Optical When your eyes itch.

Otter What water becomes as you heat it.

P

Palate What a cannibal did to his friend.

Pantry Room where you keep your slacks, jeans etc.

Pants Something a dog does and a man steps into.

Paradise Two perfect little cubes with dots on them.

Particle When your dad amuses you.

Password To hand a note to someone in class.

Pasteurize Too far away to see.

Pen pals Pigs that get along well.

Pickle Cucumber in trouble.

Pigswill How a dead pig leaves things to his family.

Propaganda Polite, well behaved male goose.

Q

Quack A duck's doctor.

Quadrant Four-sided insect.

Quake Fearful duck call.

Quality A very fine, hot beverage, especially drunk by the English.

Qualm Feeling odd about a coming storm.

Quarantine When a youth locks himself in his bedroom for months at a time.

Quay Something you need to start a motor boat.

Quicksand Beach where motor races are held.

Quickset Type of glue.

Quince Five children born at the same time.

Quota Someone who likes to report other people's speech.

R

Rabble A pile of debris left behind by a disorderly crowd.

Race The things that come out from the Sun and travel across space at an amazing speed.

Radiant A mutant bug which begins to glow after it's been exposed to atomic energy.

Raisin A very old-looking grape.

Ramification To make someone feel sheepish.

Rawhide A nudist's clothes.

Rebate Fishing term: to place another worm on the hook.

Rectify When you try to fix something, but end up wrecking it instead.

Rote Wot I dun in my eksersize buk.

Runner beans Food for athletes.

S

Sage A wise old herb.

Sand bank Where camels keep their money.

Scales Part of fish that weighs the most.

Sedate What you learn when you look at a calendar.

Shamrock A fake stone.

Sheepish Person who has the wool pulled over their eyes.

Sibling A baby sib.

Sleeping bag A nap sack.

Sourpuss Result of science experiment involving a cat and a lemon.

Square root Diced turnip.

Stabilized A horse that's been locked in.

Steel wool A robbery at a sheep farm.

T

Taciturn A very quiet vase.

Tangent A man who has been in the sun.

Telepathy Being too lazy to give your friends a call.

Thaw How your thumb feelth if you thtick a pin in it.

Thesaurus A talking dinosaur that uses big words.

Thoroughbred High-class baked goods.

Three-legged race Popular event at the Monster Olympic Games.

Toadstool Object used by a toad to repair its car.

Transistor A robot's female relative.

Transparent What mothers and fathers are when hypnotized.

U

Ultramarine The best sailor in the navy.

Unabridged A river you have to swim across.

Undercover agent A spy on a camping trip.

Unflappable A word which describes a flightless bird.

Unicorn A single blemish on the foot.

Unlucky Crossing the street to avoid walking under a ladder and getting hit by a truck full of horseshoes.

Unsavory Sweet.

Unscramble Something you can't do to an egg.

Unused A word which describes teacher's sense of humor.

Uproar What a short lion does.

V

Valid The thing on the top of a jar.

Vampire bat What Dracula uses to play baseball.

Vanish An invisible substance you paint on fences.

Varmint Troublesome candy.

Ventriloquist A man who never speaks for himself.

Veto What's on ve end of ve foot.

Victim A pair of twins in my class.

Violence Musical instruments with strings.

Viper Vhat you use to clean ze vindows.

Volcano A mountain that's blown its top.

Voltage The era that began after the discovery of electricity.

W

Waiter Someone who thinks money grows on trays.

Walkie-talkie What you get if you cross a parrot with a centipede.

Warehouse Where the wolfman lives.

Water polo What horses play in the swimming pool.

Water table Where fish eat their dinners.

Wattage Question you ask to find out how old someone is.

Whisker A chef who beats eggs.

X

X-ray My dead uncle Raymond.

Xylophone Revolutionary communication device that turns the sounds of the voice into a mellow, musical chime.

Y

Yawn A kind of heavy breathing used in school.

Yeoman A greeting you should never use for your teacher.

Yesterday The day of the week when homework's due by.

Yogurt Stretching exercise that makes you ache.

Youngish What your parents think they are.

Z

Zeal An enthusiastic sea mammal.

Zinc What a ship will do if it has a hole in it.

Zit Command given to a spotted dog.

Zoophyte What happens when captive gorillas annoy each other.

93

In summary...

Name: Mickey Mouth

Teacher's remarks:

This boy is an excellent communicator.
He never shuts up.

Name: Des Respectful

Teacher's remarks:

An independent learner.
Ignores everything I tell him.

Name: Bridget D. Fidgett

Teacher's remarks:

An active member of class.
Will not sit quietly for more than a
minute at a time.

Name: L. A. Zeebones

Teacher's remarks:

Tests do not give him any problems.
He's never shown up for one.

Name: Lynn Guist

Teacher's remarks:

Very good at using language -
the kind that earns her detention.

Name: Wayne Payne

Teacher's remarks:

He can't wait until he leaves school. Neither can we.

Name: Lou Neetunes

Teacher's remarks:

Has an excellent ear for music. Never shows up for class without his personal stereo.

Name: S. Portsman

Teacher's remarks:

Enjoys physical activity, as it doesn't involve using his mind.

Name: Amber Dextrous

Teacher's remarks:

This pupil is excellent with her hands. She's the roughest fighter in school.

Name: R. Tistic

Teacher's remarks:

His artwork was displayed all over school, until we confiscated his spray cans.

Really Awful Classroom Jokes

Our teacher talks to
herself. Does yours?

Yes, but she doesn't realize it...
she thinks we're actually listening!

Listen up, class. Tomorrow morning,
we will have only half a day of school.

Hooray!

... and we'll have the other
half day in the afternoon.

Groan!

Really Awful Classroom Jokes
CONTENTS

attention
i must pay more ~~blackbeard~~ in class
i must pay more attention in class

i must pay more attention in class

i must pay more attention in class

i must pay more attention in class

i must pay more attention in class

i must pay more attention in class

i must pay more attention in class

i must pay more attention in class

i must pay more attention in class

i must pay more attention in class

i must pay more attention in class

i must pay more attention in

class War!

mr. smith

If you add 34,312 and 76,188, divide the total by 3 and multiply it by 4, what do you get?

The wrong answer!

Teacher: Jimmy, which two words, in English, have the most letters?

Jimmy: Post Office.

Teacher: Martina, why did you say that English homework is similar to going to jail for murder?

Martina: Because they both involve long sentences!

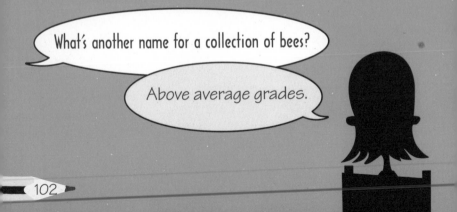

What's another name for a collection of bees?

Above average grades.

Teacher: Now, can anyone count to ten in German?

Class: Nein!

Teacher: Hmm, that's not bad for a start.

Teacher: I asked you to draw a cow eating grass. Where's the grass?

Pupil: Well, you were out of the classroom for so long that the cow ate all the grass.

Pupil: Monsieur Gaston, is it true that French teachers only eat one egg for breakfast?

Monsieur Gaston: Yes, for French people, one egg is always *un oeuf.*

Teacher: Doris, can you name something that is brown and sticky?

Doris: A stick.

Teacher: Can anybody tell me which days begin with the letter "T"?
Pupil: Me sir! "Today" and "tomorrow".

Teacher: Joey, what has wheels and flies?
Joey: A garbage truck.

How old were you on your last birthday?

Nine.

How old will you be on your next birthday?

Eleven.

That's impossible!

No it's not, I'm ten today.

Teacher: Can anybody tell me what happens to something, such as a car, when it rusts?
Pupil: Yeah, someone sells it to my dad, for our family car.

General nonsense

Which month has 28 days?

All of them.

A salary is a form of wages, where the worker is paid a guaranteed amount every month. For example, I am paid a salary. Any questions?

Yes. Where do you work, sir?

Frank, how do you manage to get so many things wrong in a day?

Because I get here so early, sir.

Can anybody tell me, what's a spaceman?

You park your car in it, man!

If you have a referee in soccer, what do you have in bowls?

Soup.

I have 100 eyes, four wings and six legs. What am I?

But miss, you have two eyes, two legs and no wings.

No, no. If I say that I have 100 eyes, four wings and six legs, what would you say that I am?

A liar, miss?

Miss Smith, does money grow on trees?

Of course not.

Then why do banks have branches?

Inglish

Joey, R-O-X does not spell rocks.

What does it spell then?

Teacher: Tracey, what's the plural of mouse?
Tracey: Mice.
Teacher: Excellent. Now, what's the plural of baby?
Tracey: Twins!

Teacher: Nicky, spell mouse.
Nicky: M-O-U-S.
Teacher: Not bad. But what's on the end?
Nicky: A tail?

Teacher: If can't is short for cannot, what is "don't" short for?
Pupil: Doughnut?

Teacher: What's the longest sentence you can think of, Frankie?

Frankie: Life imprisonment, Mr. Jones.

Teacher: Clara, I told you to write this out ten times to improve your spelling. You've only done it seven times.

Clara: Sorry, miss. My counting isn't too hot either.

Ali, name two pronouns.

Who? Me?

Teacher: What are you writing, Sarah?

Sarah: A letter to myself, sir.

Teacher: And what does it say?

Sarah: I don't know. I won't receive it till tomorrow.

Johnny, can you give me a sentence with a direct object?

You're beautiful, sir.

Thanks Johnny, but what was the object?

A good grade on my report card.

Teacher: Christopher, what word, if pronounced right, is wrong, but if pronounced wrong, is right?

Christopher: Wrong, Miss Smith.

Teacher: Right!

Teacher: What's the opposite of woe, Joe?

Joe: Giddy up!

Teacher: Today, we'll continue our reading of Shakespeare's Hamlet.

Class: But sir, our class isn't doing Hamlet.

Teacher: Oh. Is this room 2B, or not 2B?

Teacher: Martina, can you give me a sentence beginning with I?

Martina: I is the…

Teacher: No, no, no! You must always say, "I am…"

Martina: I am the ninth letter of the alphabet.

Teacher: Give me a sentence using the word "diploma".

Pupil: My water pipes burst so dad called diploma.

Teacher: Give me a sentence using the word "fascinate".

Pupil: I have a coat with nine buttons, but I can only fascinate.

Teacher: Give me a sentence using the word "information".

Pupil: Geese sometimes fly information.

In the lab

Name a liquid that doesn't freeze.

Hot water!

Teacher: How many planets are there out in space?

Class: All of them.

Teacher: What's the most important lesson you learn in chemistry class, Stan?

Stan: Never lick the spoon!

Teacher: How do you make a science teacher into a mad scientist?

Pupil: Er, step on her toes?

Teacher: How do you prevent diseases caused by biting insects?

Pupil: Don't bite insects, sir.

Teacher: What's the chemical formula for water?

Pupil: H-I-J-K-L-M-N-O.

Teacher: No, of course not!

Pupil: But last week you told us that the chemical formula for water is H_2O.

Teacher: I'm going to give you all a chemistry exercise for your homework.

Class: Cool! Will we be pumping ions?

What is claustrophobia?

Fear of Santa Claus.

Teacher: What happened when electricity was first discovered?
Pupil: Somebody got a very bad shock, sir.

Teacher: Carrie, can you name four members of the cat family?
Carrie: A mother cat, a father cat, and two kittens.

What has big ears and a trunk?

A mouse on vacation.

Teacher: If I were to say that I was the planet Neptune, and that this desk is the Sun, and then I started running around the desk, what would you say I was doing?
Pupil: Going crazy, sir?

Teacher: If you pull the wings off a fly, what happens?

Pupil: It becomes a walk.

William, besides wood, can you name a poor conductor?

The music teacher, sir.

Teacher: How can you prove that the Earth is round, Billy?

Billy: Please, sir, I never said that it was.

Teacher: Tell me how we can keep milk from turning sour.

Pupil: Leave it in the cow, sir.

Teacher: Today we'll be learning about electricity.

Class: Cool. Maybe you'll say something shocking.

Geography

Teacher: Where are the Great Plains of North America?

Class: In an aviation museum!

Teacher: Rosie, can you name two French wine growing regions.

Rosie: Red and white, sir.

Teacher: Carrie, which country do you like best?

Carrie: Azerbaijan.

Teacher: Can you spell it, please?

Carrie: I've changed my mind. France!

Teacher: What should you do if it rains cats and dogs?

Pupil: Take care not to stand in a poodle.

Teacher: Where are the Andes, Tracey?

Tracey: At the end of your sleevees?

Teacher: Today, I'm going to instruct you on the Alps.

Class: Wow. Will we be back for lunch?

Teacher: Find Australia on the map for me, Fred.

Fred: There it is, Miss Smith.

Teacher: Now, can anyone tell me who discovered Australia?

Another pupil: Fred did.

What is so unusual about Mississippi?

Um... it's got four eyes but it can't see a thing.

Music to your ears

Why is the music teacher holding a shoe to his ear?

Because today's lesson is about soul music.

Teacher: If "f" means *forte*, what does "ff" stand for?

Pupil: Eighty?

Teacher: Wendy, you've been practicing the violin for eight years now, and you still can't hit a note.

Wendy: But just now told me that I don't have to blow it!

Teacher: Stan, stop playing that trumpet, you're driving me crazy!

Stan: I think you might be crazy already…
I stopped ten minutes ago.

Pupil: How can I improve my guitar playing, Mr. Lee?

Mr. Lee: Leave it in its case.

Pupil: Hey, sir, what fish do piano menders like most?

Teacher: Tuna, of course!

Pupil: Miss Smith, is a tuba bad for your teeth?

Miss Smith: Not if it's a tuba toothpaste it isn't.

Pupil: Miss, what happens if you drop a piano down a mine shaft?

Teacher: It makes A-flat minor, of course.

In Ancient Egypt, what music did the mummies like most?

WRaP MuSic

You said I'd be able to learn the violin in six easy lessons.

I did... But I didn't mention the 500 very difficult ones that followed.

Pupil: Mr. Lee, why *do* you suddenly have such a high singing voice?

Mr. Lee: I can't help it, it's my falsetto teeth.

Drums teacher: Why did you say you envy me?

Science teacher: Because you're allowed to tell your pupils to "beat it"!

Pupil: What music did people listen to when they built Stonehenge, sir?

Teacher: Heavy rock, I'd imagine!

Pupil: Why are opera singers afraid of cruise ships?

Teacher: Because they don't like the high Cs.

Teacher: Laura, how can you tell when your violin is out of tune?

Laura: It's easy, I just move the bow across the strings.

Teacher: Why are you all cheering?

Class: We just realized that the piano's locked.

Teacher: Then I'll sing until I find the right key!

Teacher: Anyone here any good at picking up music?

Nicky: Me, me, me!

Teacher: Great! Move that piano.

Completely mental arithmetic

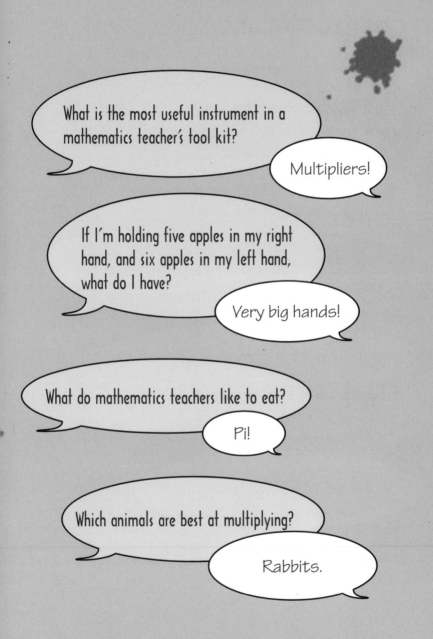

What is the most useful instrument in a mathematics teacher's tool kit?

Multipliers!

If I'm holding five apples in my right hand, and six apples in my left hand, what do I have?

Very big hands!

What do mathematics teachers like to eat?

Pi!

Which animals are best at multiplying?

Rabbits.

Teacher: Why do you wish you lived 200 years ago, Michael?

Michael: We wouldn't have so much history to learn, would we?

Teacher: Joseph, how long did Isaac Newton live?

Joseph: All his life, Mrs. Harris.

Teacher: Karen, when did Julius Caesar die?

Karen: A few days before his funeral?

Teacher: Why did you say that Rome was built at night?

Pupil: Because my dad told me that it wasn't built in a day.

Teacher: When I was at school, the subject I liked best was history.

Pupil: Excuse me, sir, wasn't it called current affairs in those days?

Teacher: How did ancient warriors learn their skills?

Pupil: At knight school!

Teacher: Frankie, do you know why George Washington was buried at Mount Vernon?

Frankie: Because he was dead, I reckon.

Name something important that didn't exist 100 years ago.

The modern world, miss.

Class wildlife

Teacher: If a flea was as big as a man, it could jump higher than a house. Why are you laughing, Don?

Don: Sir, houses can't jump!

Teacher: Can anybody tell me how animals in Africa know when it is time to migrate?

Pupil: Is it because they keep an eye on the gnus, sir?

Teacher: In this box, I have a ten foot snake. Why are you all laughing?

Class: Because snakes don't have feet, sir.

Meanwhile, in computer class...

How can you tell when a teacher's been using a computer?

There's correction fluid all over the screen.

Why is the computer teacher so tired?

Because she took a hard drive to work.

What food do computer teachers like most?

Chips.

What's the best way to break a computer?

Let a grown up use it.

There was an old teacher named Green,

Who invented a caning machine,

On the ninety-ninth stroke

The rotten thing broke

And made that cruel man a has-been.

Danny, where is your homework?

This is <u>not</u> an essay.

Please <u>see me</u>!

You're
in Trouble

You're in trouble

Sam! Are you copying Adam's answers?

No sir, I'm just checking to see if he's got his right.

Edward, go and stand outside the principal's study!

What for?

The rest of the class.

This is the third time I've had to speak to you this week. What do you have to say about that?

I say thank goodness it's Friday, Miss Smith.

Parent-teacher night

Teacher: With grades like these, there's only one thing I can say about your daughter, Mr. Brown.

Mr. Brown: What's that?

Teacher: She can't be cheating.

Parent: I'm outraged! I want to take my daughter out of this terrible mathematics class.

Teacher: But she's at the top of her class.

Parent: Exactly!

Teacher: Mrs. Frost, last year you were worried that your son was going to fail.

Mrs. Frost: Yes, I remember.

Teacher: Well, your worries are over.

Teacher: Congratulations, Mrs. Clark. Your son has finally moved up from kindergarten. How does he feel?

Mrs. Clark: He's delighted. In fact, he was so excited he cut himself shaving.

Teacher: Your daughter is a wonder child, Mr. Day.

Mr. Day: Oh, that is good to know.

Teacher: Yes, I wonder if she ever listens to a thing I say.

Teacher: Your daughter's writing has improved 100% this year, Mrs. Lowe.

Mrs. Lowe: Excellent. I'm so pleased.

Teacher: The only problem is... now I can see all the spelling mistakes.

Teacher: Frank Smith is the stupidest boy in the class.

Mr. Smith: Oi! That's my son you're talking about!

Teacher: Oh, I'm sorry!

Mr. Smith: So am I. I have to live with him.

You're late

An old physics teacher named Bright,

Once managed to go faster than light,

He started one day

In the relative way

And returned on the previous night.

Charles Applethwait

What's your name?

Roll call

Teacher: What is your name?

Pupil: Al, sir.

Teacher: Al who?

Pupil: Al be asleep by the end of the roll call.

Teacher: King, Joseph.

Pupil: Here, sir.

Teacher: Hey, you must be "joking"! Ha-ha!

Pupil: Very funny, Mr. Cook.

Teacher: Name?

Pupil: Albie.

Teacher: Albie who?

Pupil: Albie blowed, you forgot my name.

Teacher: What is your name?

Pupil: Ariel.

Teacher: Ariel pain in the neck?

Pupil: No, Ariel joy to teach, that's me!

trouble

Teacher: Name?

Pupil: Liz.

Teacher: Liz who?

Pupil: Liz-en more carefully, I told you my name yesterday.

Teacher: What's your name?

Pupil: Karen, sir.

Teacher: Karen who?

Pupil: Karen you recognize me?

Teacher: And what's your name?

Pupil: Sarah.

Teacher: Sarah who?

Pupil: Sarah easy way to pass today's test?

Teacher: Name?

Pupil: Don Juan.

Teacher: Don Juan who?

Pupil: Don Juan to be in zees school today.

Teacher: Your name, please.

Pupil: Don.

Teacher: Don who?

Pupil: Don you know my name yet?

Teacher: Your name?

Pupil: Edward.

Teacher: Edward who?

Pupil: Edward be nice if you let us go home early today.

Teacher: Name?

Pupil: Dawn.

Teacher: Dawn who?

Pupil: Dawn you get sick of doing roll call, day in and day out?

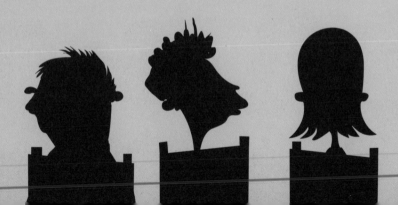

Teacher: Name?

Pupil: Harry.

Teacher: Harry who?

Pupil: Harry up and get on with the lesson, sir!

Teacher: Name?

Pupil: Wendy.

Teacher: Wendy who?

Pupil: Wendy teacher's back
is turned, we all make faces.

Teacher: Name?

Pupil: Alfie.

Teacher: Alfie who?

Pupil: Oh not again... Alfie give your
forgetfulness, I know you're getting old.

The principal's office

Principal: So, you've been causing trouble. What's your name?

Pupil: Danielle.

Principal: Danielle who?

Pupil: Danielle at me, I've done nothing wrong.

Principal: So, you've been giving silly excuses to your teacher! What's your name?

Pupil: Alma.

Principal: Alma who?

Pupil: Alma homework got eaten by the dog, honestly.

Principal: I want you to tell me who broke the window. First, tell me your name.

Pupil: Doris.

Principal: Doris who?

Pupil: Doris no way I'm telling you anything.

Principal: Hmm, it appears I punished you by mistake last week. What's your name again?

Pupil: Aaron.

Principal: Aaron who?

Pupil: Aaron you going to say sorry to me?

Principal: Who are you?

Pupil: Noah, sir.

Principal: Noah who?

Pupil: Noah good joke, sir? I could do with a laugh!

Principal: The teacher sent you to see me because you didn't do your homework. What's your name?

Pupil: Alex.

Principal: Alex who?

Pupil: Alex-plain later. Can I go now?

Principal: And what is your name?

Pupil: Hutch.

Principal: Really? Hutch who?

Pupil: Bless you, sir.

Principal: You look upset. What's your name?

Pupil: Celeste.

Principal: Celeste who?

Pupil: Celeste time I saw a face like yours, I cried. Boo-hoo!

Principal: Name, boy.

Pupil: Frank Lee.

Principal: Frank Lee who?

Pupil: Frank Lee it's none of your business.

Principal: Who are you?
You act like you own the place.

Pupil: Alex.

Principal: Alex who?

Pupil: Look, Alex the
questions around here. Got that?

Principal: So, the terrible twins from Mr. Lee's class have been sent
to me. Now, remind me of your names.

Twins: Harv and Hugh.

Principal: Harv and Hugh who?

Twins: Harv and Hugh got better things to do
than ask us silly questions?

Principal: For the last time, I demand you tell me your name.
There'll be trouble if you don't.

Pupil: Sadie.

Principal: Sadie who?

Pupil: Sadie magic word and then
I'll tell you.

A knock at the staffroom door

Knock knock!

Teacher: Who's there?

Pupil: Howell.

Teacher: Howell who?

Pupil: Howell you find out if you don't open the door?

Knock knock!

Teacher: Who's there?

Pupil: Hugo.

Teacher: Hugo who?

Pupil: Hugoing to let me in or what?

Knock knock!

Teacher: Who's there?

Pupil: Carrie.

Teacher: Carrie who?

Pupil: Carrie me up to see the nurse, I've hurt my leg.

Knock knock!

Teacher: Who's there?

Pupil: Ivan.

Teacher: Ivan who?

Pupil: Ivan to go home, please.

Knock knock!

Teacher: Who's there?

Pupil: Eileen.

Teacher: Eileen who?

Pupil: Eileen on your car and, guess what, it dents. Oops!

Knock knock!

Teacher: Who's there?

Pupil 1: Oscar...

Pupil 2: ...and Greta.

Teacher: Oscar and Greta who?

Pupil 1: Oscar stupid question...

Pupil 2: ...and Greta silly answer.

A right-handed teacher named Wright,
Wrote "rite" when she meant to write "right".
If she'd written right well
She'd have shown she could spell
And not written rot writing right.

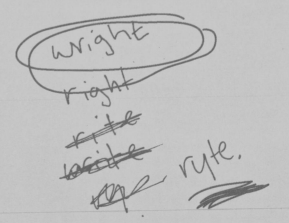

Not so smart

Teacher: James, you've been cheating.

James: How did you know?

Teacher: Well, where Bill's answer says "I don't know!" you put "Me neither!"

Teacher: Kevin, your ideas are like flawless diamonds.

Kevin: Thank you sir. Is that because they are so brilliant and valuable?

Teacher: No, it's because they are so rare.

Pupil: Mr. Lee, does ham grow on trees?

Mr. Lee: Of course not.

Pupil: Well, what's an ambush then?

Teacher: Jane, how did you manage to get all those splinters in your hand?

Jane: I don't know, miss. I just scratched my head.

Pupil: When I grow up I'm going to be a cop and follow in my father's footsteps.

Teacher: I'm glad to hear that, but I didn't know your dad was a police officer.

Pupil: He's not, he's a burglar.

Teacher: How do dolphins stay in touch?

Pupil: They send sea mails to each other!

Teacher: What's that you're reading, Edward?

Edward: Don't know, sir.

Teacher: But you're reading out loud.

Edward: Yeah, but I'm not listening.

Teacher: Karen, what on earth are you doing standing on your head?

Karen: Well you just told us to turn things over in our minds.

Teacher: Where are my glasses?

Pupil: You're sitting on them, sir.

Teacher: Aargh. Why didn't you tell me before?

Pupil: Well I didn't think you'd want them if they were broken.

Pupil: I keep thinking I'm a dog.

Teacher: Oh, don't be so ridiculous. Now go back to your desk and sit down.

Pupil: I can't, sir. I'm not allowed on the furniture.

Pupil: Is it true that the number nine no longer exists?

Teacher: Of course not. What made you think that?

Pupil: Well, I'm sure I heard you say "seven ate nine".

Teacher: Danielle, you never get anything right. What on earth are you going to do when you leave school?

Danielle: I thought I'd become a TV weather girl. They never get anything right, either.

Pupil: Why *do* you keep calling me squirrel, sir?

Teacher: Because you drive me nuts.

Pupil: Why *do* you keep calling me big cat, Mrs. Harris?

Mrs. Harris: Because I've come to the conclusion that you're a cheater.

Pupil: Mr. Cook, is the English Royal Family stupid?

Mr. Cook: Certainly not! Why do you ask?

Pupil: Well why did they build Windsor Castle so close to Heathrow airport?

Silly teachers

How old do you think the history teacher is?

At least 40. Because my brother's 20 and the history teacher is twice as annoying as my brother.

Ask the teacher what worms taste like.

Why? How will she know?

Because there was one in the apple that I just gave her.

What's the difference between a dull teacher and a dull book?

You can shut the book up!

Why does that teacher wear dark glasses?

Because he likes to keep his pupils in the dark.

Did you hear that our nutty science teacher has taken down his front doorbell?

Yeah. He's obsessed with winning the no-bell prize.

Why did you just call the dullest teacher in the school "absolutely fascinating"?

Because he's standing behind you, right now!

How many jokes about silly teachers are there?

None! They're all true.

Don't say this about teacher

She's an experiment in Artifical Stupidity.

He's a few clowns short of a circus.

He's a few straws shy of a bale.

She's a few yards short of the hole.

The wheel's spinning, but the hamster's dead.

Her receiver's off the hook.

He's all wax and no wick.

She's a few sandwiches short of a picnic.

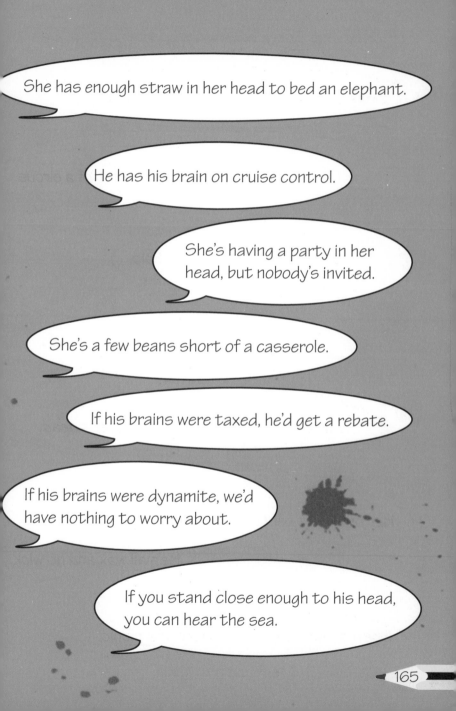

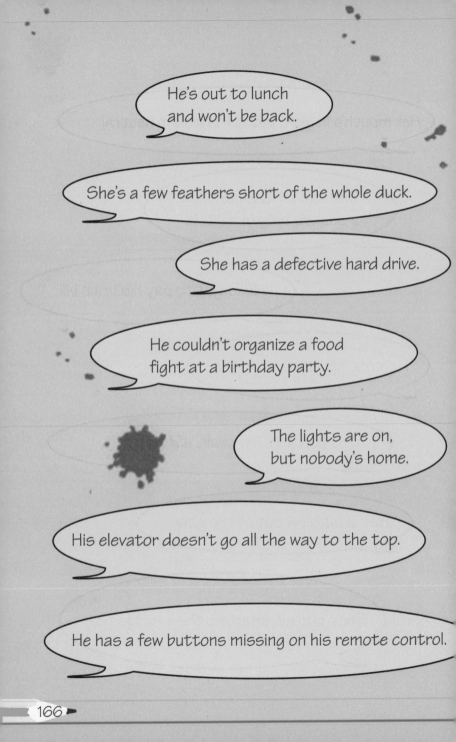

Her mouth's in gear, but her brain's in neutral.

She has an IQ lower than a snake's belly in a ditch.

He forgot to pay his brain bill.

He's one bit short of a byte.

If he had another brain, it'd be lonely.

He's a bit slow out of the gate.

She's not as smart as the average bear.

A peculiar teacher named Ray,
Used to teach in a very odd way,
He gave lessons in verse
But it made matters worse
So the moral is: rhymes just don't pay!

school food and and sickness

Lunchtime

Pupil: Yuck! There's a fly in my soup.

Cook: Shush, you'll make the other kids jealous.

Pupil: Oh no, what's this fly doing in my soup?

Cook: Looks like it's drowning, to me.

Pupil: Oh no! I've got a fly in my soup, too!

Cook: You're mistaken. That's a cockroach.

Jim: What has eyes but can't see?

Jane: A school lunchroom potato.

Tom: What do school cheese and our school cook's nose have in common?

Tim: They both smell, and they're both runny.

Teacher: Clara, if you take a pie from the school lunchroom and eat three-quarters, what are you left with?

Clara: Stomachache.

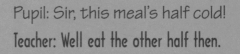

Pupil: Sir, this meal's half cold!

Teacher: Well eat the other half then.

Pupil: Sir, you just sat on some grapes.

Teacher: Ah, I thought I just heard something let out a little wine.

Teacher: Why did you say that school cooks are even crueller than teachers?

Pupil: Because they batter fish, beat eggs and whip cream.

Charlie: I wonder why school meat is so tough.

Mike: I'm not sure, but I heard the cook say that it was full of iron.

Teacher: You've got your finger in my soup!

Pupil: It's okay, it isn't hot.

Pupil: What's the difference between school lunches and fresh horse droppings?

Teacher: Not much, except that one is fresher and warmer than the other.

Zoë: Why do you think the school basketball team make such a mess when they eat?

Chloë: Because they all like to dribble.

Pupil: This food must be really clean, you know.

Teacher: Why's that?

Pupil: Because it tastes like soap!

Pupil: What kind of pie is this? It tastes like glue.

Cook: That would be the apple pie. The plum pie tastes like paint.

New girl: Why is the school nurse's office next to the school lunchroom?

New girl's friend: Taste the food, then you'll find out.

Pupil: These peas are as hard as bullets.

Teacher: Let me taste them.... Hmm, they seem soft enough to me!

Pupil: Well they would, I've been chewing them for the last half an hour.

Problems, problems

Mr. Lee, I feel as if everyone's ignoring me.

Now you know how I feel.

Pupil: Help, I need to see the nurse, I've only got 60 seconds to live.

Teacher: Just wait a minute, please, Johnny.

Teacher: Good grief, Wendy, what are you taking for that cough?

Wendy: How much will you give me for it, sir?

Pupil: Please miss, I have a problem. Could you help me out?

Teacher: Yes, I'll hold the door for you.

Pupil: Can I go and see the nurse, please? I think I'm turning into a garbage can.

Teacher: Don't talk trash.

Pupil: Miss Smith, I'm so tired but I can't sleep. What should I do?

Miss Smith: Lie on the edge of your bed, and you'll soon drop off.

Please can I go and see the nurse? I think I've turned invisible.

I'm sorry, I don't think she'll be able to see you just now.

Mrs. Harris, the other kids say I've turned into a pig.

Oh, go and see the nurse. She'll give you some oinkment.

Pupil: Help me, Mr. Jones. I've just swallowed a roll of film.

Mr. Jones: Just go and sit in a darkened room. We'll wait and see what develops.

Help, I've lost my memory.

When did this happen?

When did what happen?

Pupil: Please miss, there's something wrong with me. I can see into the future.

Teacher: That's amazing. When did this start?

Pupil: Next Thursday.

Pupil: Oh Mr. Lee. I've cut myself really badly.

Mr. Lee: Well, just listen to this joke, it'll have you in stitches.

Pupil: Miss, I keep thinking that there's two of me.

Teacher: For goodness sake, one at a time please.

Restaurant

Pupil: Teacher, teacher, I keep getting lost. I can never find the right room for my classes.

Waiter: You do have a problem, young lady. This is a restaurant.

Pupil: Mr. Cook, I keep thinking I'm a little birdie.

Mr. Cook: Go and see the nurse right away. She'll give you some tweatment.

Pupil: Mr. Lee. I think I'm shrinking.

Mr. Lee: Well, go and wait at the nurse's office, and be a little patient.

Teacher: My, you look tired Joey.

Joey: Oh, the problem is that I snore so loudly I wake myself up.

Teacher: Well, sleep in another room then.

Miss Smith, I feel like a deck of cards.

Go and sit down, I'll deal with you later. And for goodness sake, stop shuffling.

Pupil: Mr. Lee, I feel like a car.
Can I go and see the nurse?

Mr. Lee: Yes, you do look tired, and exhausted.

Why am I covered in wheel marks, Miss Smith?

Well, it looks to me as if you've allowed yourself to get run down.

Pupil: Oh Mr. Cook, I don't feel well. My nose keeps running and my feet smell.

Mr. Cook: Hmm. You'd better go and see the nurse. It looks to me as if life has turned you upside down.

Sir, I think your face looks like a clock.

You're just trying to wind me up.

In the old days a teacher named Bind,

Gave my dad, in a manner unkind,

Heavy whacks to the head

With a flat piece of lead

Saying "This lesson will broaden your mind!"

Teacher's car

A teacher walks into a service station and asks the mechanic:

Could you get a headlight for my car?

The mechanic walks around the car, scratches his head, thinks a little, and then says:

I'm not sure that's a fair trade, you know...

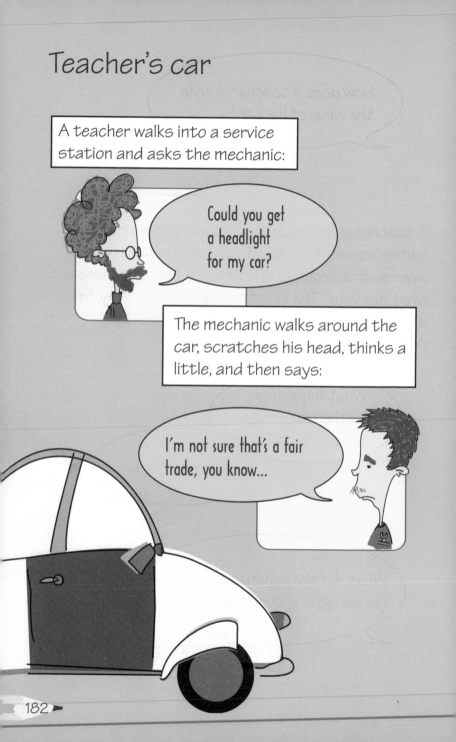

How *does* a teacher double the value of his car?

He fills the tank up.

A teacher is driving along a country road. He comes across a donkey. The donkey, never having seen such a decrepit vehicle, says, "My goodness, what are you?" The teacher's car replies, "Why, I'm a car, of course." The donkey says, "Yeah right. And I'm a horse."

What happened to the carpentry teacher's car?

Wooden start!

What did the teacher say when his car got to the top of the hill?

It's a miracle!

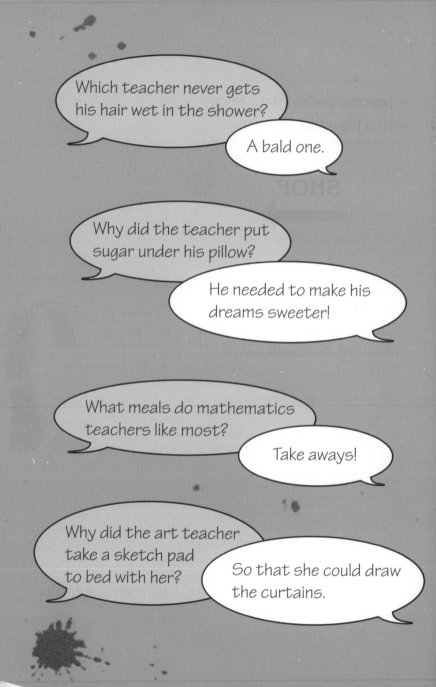

Which teacher never gets his hair wet in the shower?

A bald one.

Why did the teacher put sugar under his pillow?

He needed to make his dreams sweeter!

What meals do mathematics teachers like most?

Take aways!

Why did the art teacher take a sketch pad to bed with her?

So that she could draw the curtains.

Look who's talking!

A teacher walks into a shop with a pig under his arm...

SHOP →

A store clerk walks over.

My, that's the ugliest animal I've ever seen. Where on earth did you get it?

I won him in a raffle.

Home time

Pupil: Dad, I saved some money today. I resisted the temptation to catch the bus and walked home instead.

Pupil's dad: Why didn't you resist the temptation to catch a taxi? You'd have saved more.

My teacher was doing bird impressions today.

Oh really, how nice. What did she do?

She watched me like a hawk.

Pupil: Today, my teacher asked me if I have any younger brothers or sisters who will be coming to my school.

Pupil's mother: That's nice of her, dear. But did you tell her that you are an only child?

Pupil: Yes. She said, "Thank goodness!"

Pupil's dad: What did you learn at school today, son?

Pupil: I learned that the homework you did for me was all wrong!

What are you going to do this evening?

I'm going to help my dad with my homework.

Pupil: Oh dear, I had a terrible day at school. The other girls all said I have big feet.

Pupil's mother: That's nonsense.

Pupil: And there's a school skiing trip, but you said last year that we couldn't afford skis.

Pupil's mother: That's no problem, I'm sure you'll just be able to use your shoes.

End of term report

189

Teacher's worst jokes

How was the naughty train punished?

It had to write railway lines.

Why did the toad visit the mushroom?

He thought it was a toad-school.

Which English king was good at fractions?

Henry the Eighth.

What disease do art teachers get?

Pencilitis.

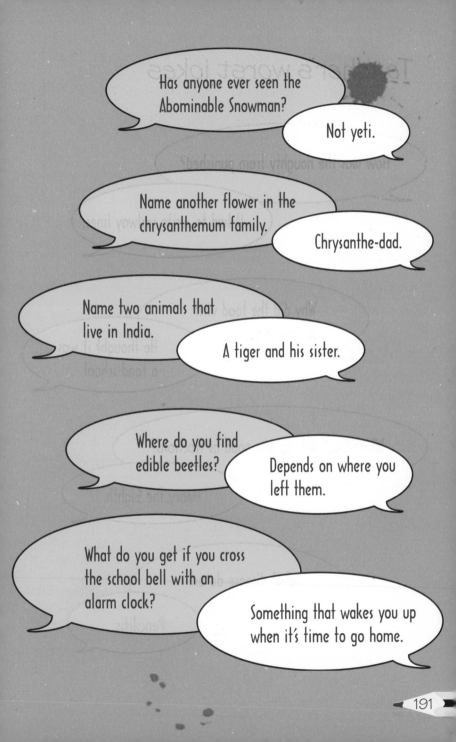

Really silly
Jokes

Really Silly Jokes

CONTENTS

AROUND THE WORLD

Down under

What's Australia's most popular drink?
Coca-Koala.

What's the scariest part of Australia?
The Northern Terror-tory.

How do you describe an
exhausted kangaroo?
Out of bounds.

What do you call a boomerang
that doesn't come back?
A stick.

What famous story was about an
Australian reptile?
The Lizard of Oz.

Why do mother koalas carry their babies?
**Because the babies are too small to carry
the mothers.**

What do you get if you cross a kangaroo
with an elephant?
Huge potholes all over Australia.

What's purple and furry?
A kangaroo holding its breath.

North America

What is white, furry and found in Florida?
A polar bear with a bad sense of direction.

What American city do cows live in?
Moo York.

Knock knock.

Who's there?

Alaska.

Alaska who?

Alaska again, will you please open the door?

What is the capital of Canada?
C.

Where do you find Quebec?
On a map.

What holiday do American vampires celebrate?
Fangsgiving.

What stands in New York and sneezes all day?
The a-choo of Liberty.

What would you get if you crossed a
gorilla with an American president?
Ape-raham Lincoln.

Who was America's first animated president?
George Washingtoon.

Europe

Why is Europe like a frying pan?
Because it has Greece at the bottom.

Why did the Irishman go to the foot doctor?
He had lepre-corns.

How do you make a Venetian blind?
Poke him in the eye.

What's tall, Italian and covered in pepperoni?
The leaning tower of Pizza.

Why should you be worried if you eat bad
food in Germany?
Because the wurst is yet to come.

dot

dot   *dash*

What happened to the Frenchman who fell into the river in Paris?
He was declared in-Seine.

Where's the best place in Europe to find sharks?
Finland.

What does a Spanish farmer say to his hens?
Olé!

Where was the Queen of England crowned?
On her head.

How did Vikings send secret messages?
By Norse code.

dot dot

dash

Out of this world

What kind of music can you hear in space?
A Nep-tune.

What sea is in space?
The galax-sea.

How do you get a baby astronaut to sleep?
Rocket.

What do you call a wizard in outer space?
A flying sorcerer.

Where do astronauts leave their spaceships?
At parking meteors.

What did one shooting star say to the other?
Pleased to meteor.
Did you hear about the space shuttle that collided with the Dog Star?
It made a mess, but nothing Sirius.
When do astronauts eat their sandwiches?
At launch time.

All at sea

What can fly underwater?
A parrot in a submarine.

What's the best way to communicate with a fish?
Drop it a line.

How do fish get to school?
By octobus.

What do you call a stupid squid?
A squidiot.

Why are goldfish orange?

Because the water
turns us rusty.

Why did the fish take an aspirin?
Because it had a haddock.

What sits on the
seabed and shakes?
A nervous wreck.

What kind of fish
only swims at night?
A starfish.

All over the place

What do you say if someone tells a lie in South America?

I don't Bolivia.

Why do Egyptian pyramids have doorbells?

So you can toot-'n'-come-in.

What do you find in the middle of Japan?

The letter "p".

How would you describe the rain in Spain?

Little drops of water falling from the sky.

209

There was a young zombie named Khan,
Who was known for his kindness and charm.
If a stranger or friend
Ever needed a hand,
He'd give them a leg or an arm.

Fang-tastic!

What movie do vampires like best?
Batman.

What kind of coffee does Dracula drink?
Decoffinated.

What kind of mail does a famous vampire get?
Fang mail.

Who did Dracula get engaged to?
His girl-fiend.

What do you get if you meet Dracula in the middle of winter?
Frostbite.

What happened to the vampires who wanted to make a movie?
They couldn't find a good crypt writer.

What kind of jewels do vampires wear?
Tomb stones.

Why do people hate being bitten by vampires?
Because it's a drain in the neck.

What does a vampire bathe in?
A bat tub.

Why are vampires like false teeth?
They come out at night.

Hairy and scary

What does a werewolf write at the end of a letter?
"Best vicious"

Why did the werewolf buy two tickets at the zoo?
One to get in and one to get out.

What do you call a dentist who
treats werewolves?
Brave.

What happened when the
werewolf swallowed a clock?

He got ticks.

What did the zombie get a medal for?
Deadication.

What does a little zombie call his parents?
Mummy and Deady.

What do you call twin zombies in a belfry?
Dead ringers.

Where do zombies go on vacation?
The Deaditerranean.

Why did the doctor tell the zombie to take a rest?

He was dead on his feet.

Frankie panky

Why did Frankenstein's monster get indigestion?

He bolted down his food.

What happened when Frankenstein's monster swallowed some plutonium?

He got atomic ache.

I heard Dr. Frankenstein is going to marry the invisible woman.

I don't know what he sees in her.

What should you do if you find yourself surrounded by Frankenstein's monster, Count Dracula and the wolfman?

Hope you're at a Halloween party.

What was written on Frankenstein's
monster's grave?
"Rust in peace"

Why was Dr. Frankenstein never lonely?
He was good at making friends.

What do you call a clever monster?
Frank Einstein.

What did Frankenstein's monster
say to the screwdriver?
"Daddy!"

What's the best way to speak
to Frankenstein's monster?
From a distance.

Ghoulish giggles

Who protects the shores where ghosts live?
The ghost guard.

When does a ghost eat breakfast?
In the moaning.

What do you get when you cross Bambi with a ghost?
Bam-boo.

What do you call a ghost's mother and father?
Trans-parents.

When do ghosts usually appear?
Just before someone screams.

Who's the world's most famous ghost detective?
Sherlock Moans.

Hag gags

Why do witches buy magazines?
They like to read the horrorscopes.

What happened to the naughty little witch
at school?
She was ex-spelled.

What do you call a witch who drives really badly?
A road hag.

What do you call an old hag who lives by the sea?
A sandwitch.

Who went into a witch's den and came out alive?
The witch.

How do you know a witch is really ugly?
When a wasp stings her, it closes its eyes.

What do you call a witch with one leg?
Eileen.

Why do witches only ride their
broomsticks after dark?
That's the time to go to sweep.

What do witches put on their hair?
Scare spray.

What did the witch do when her broomstick broke?
She witch-hiked.

What does a witch ask for when she's in a hotel?
Broom service.

Funny bones

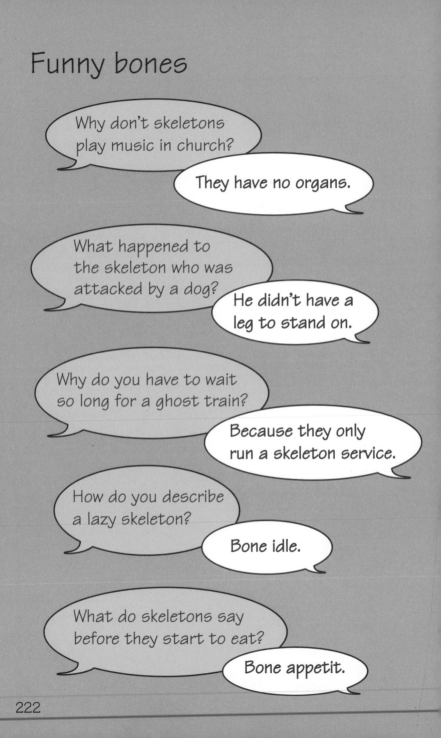

Why don't skeletons play music in church?

They have no organs.

What happened to the skeleton who was attacked by a dog?

He didn't have a leg to stand on.

Why do you have to wait so long for a ghost train?

Because they only run a skeleton service.

How do you describe a lazy skeleton?

Bone idle.

What do skeletons say before they start to eat?

Bone appetit.

Why did the skeleton go to the
Chinese restaurant?
To buy some spare ribs.

Why didn't the skeleton go skydiving?
He didn't have the guts.

Who was the most famous French skeleton?
Napoleon Bone-apart.

M-m-monsters!

What does a polite monster say when he meets you for the first time?
Pleased to eat you!

When are monsters most likely to eat people?
On Chewsday.

How do you know if a monster has a glass eye?
When it comes out in conversation.

Did you hear about the monster who had eight arms?
He said they came in handy.

Where are yetis found?
They're so big, they're hardly ever lost.

How does a yeti get to work?
By icicle.

What do you do with a blue monster?
Try to cheer him up.

Why did the bride of Frankenstein get squeezed to death?
He had a crush on her.

What do you call a monster with 100 children?
Dad.

If a stork brings human babies, what brings monster babies?
A crane.

An Italian girl known as Mona,
Told jokes that would make
people groan-a.
Though the gags made her smile,
Her friends ran a mile
And she ended up laughing alone-a.

Classic Jokes

... a computer with a banana skin?
A slipped disk.

... a snowman with a witch?
A cold spell.

... a big ape with a plane?
King Kongcorde.

... a muppet with a tree?
Kermit the log.

... a lake with a leaky boat?

About halfway.

What's the difference...

... between an oak tree and a tight shoe?
One make acorns, the other makes corns ache.

... between a hungry man and a greedy man?
One longs to eat and the other eats too long.

... between a fly and a bird?
A bird can fly, but a fly can't bird.

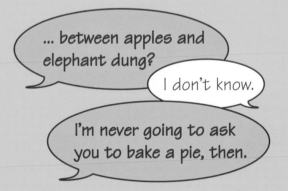

... between apples and elephant dung?

I don't know.

I'm never going to ask you to bake a pie, then.

... between a crazy dog and a short-sighted teacher?
One barks madly and the other marks badly.

... between a big hill and a big pill?
One's hard to get up, the other's hard to get down.

... between an overweight person and a bored guest?
One's going to diet and the other's dying to go.

... between a wet day
and a lion with toothache?

One pours with rain,
the other roars with pain.

... two men who hang over a window?

Kurt 'n' Rod.

... a man who sits near a door?
Matt.

... a man with a shovel on his head?
Doug.

... a boy with a paper bag on his head?
Russell.

... a man with a car on his head?
Jack.

... a man with a bus on his head?
The **deceased**.

Knock knock!

Knock knock.

Who's there?

Dishwasher.

Dishwasher who?

Dishwasher way I shpoke when I losht my falsh teef.

Knock knock.

Who's there?

Lettuce.

Lettuce who?

Lettuce in and I'll tell you.

Knock knock.

Who's there?

Ammonia.

Ammonia who?

Ammonia little boy, I can't reach the doorbell.

237

Crossing the road

Why did the cow cross the road?
To get to the udder side.

Why did the vampire cross the road?
To get to the blood bank.

Why did the chicken cross the building site?
She wanted to see a man laying bricks.

Why did the chicken cross the road, roll
in a muddy puddle and cross the road again?
Because she was a dirty double-crosser.

DANGER!

WILD ANIMALS

ENTER AT OWN RISK

Crazy critters

Where would you find a tortoise with no legs?
Where you left it.

What sort of fish would you find in a bird cage?
A perch.

Where do rabbits go when they get married?
On their bunnymoon.

What's the largest kind of ant in the world?
An elephant.

In the wild

Why are giraffes so slow to apologize?

It takes them a long time to swallow their pride.

Why does a tiger have stripes?

So it won't be spotted.

How do you fix a broken chimp?

With a monkey wrench.

What type of lion will never eat you?

A dandelion.

Down on the farm

What do you call a tall building that's full of pigs?
A sty-scraper.

How do you hire a horse?
Put it on stilts.

How many sheep does it take
to make a sweater?
None, sheep can't knit.

What goes "aaab-aaab"?
A sheep in reverse.

What's the best cure for chicken pox?
Henicillin.

What do you get if you cross a cow with an octopus?
An animal that milks itself.

Did you hear about the tractor with the wooden wheels and the wooden engine?
It wooden go.

What does a pig use to write letters?
A pen and oink.

What game do horses like to play?
Stable tennis.

What has feathers and haunts the farmyard?
A goost.

How do sheep keep warm in winter?

Central bleating.

Why did the foal cough?
Because it was a little hoarse.

What do you get when you cross a cat with a tree?

A cat-a-log.

What kind of food do Chinese cats like to eat?

Egg fried mice.

What do you get if you cross a cat with a bat?

A cat flap.

What do you get if you cross a tomcat with a Pekingese?

A Peking Tom.

What do you call an upper-class feline?

An aristocat.

What's green and jumps out of planes with a gun?
A parrot-trooper.

What do birds like to watch after the News?
The feather forecast.

What do roosters use to wake up at dawn?

An alarm cluck.

What goes "quick quick"?
A duck with hiccups.

Creepy crawlies

Did you hear about the two silkworms who had a race?

It ended in a tie.

What did the flea say to the other flea?

Shall we walk or take the cat?

What's the world's largest moth?

A mam-moth.

What flies, has stripes and is very clumsy?

A fumble bee.

How do you tell which end of a worm is which?

Tickle the middle and see which end laughs.

How do you describe a very cold flea?
Flea-zing.

What do bees say when they get back from work?

Honey, I'm home.

What did the priest say when he saw a fly?
Let us spray.

Did you hear about the smart leech?
He was no sucker.

If bees make honey, what do wasps make?

Waspberry jam.

Funny Business

Making a living

Why did the baker stop making donuts?
He was sick of the hole business.

What's purple and fixes pipes?
A plum-er.

What's the difference between a night watchman and a butcher?
One stays awake, the other weighs a steak.

Did you hear about the plastic surgeon?
He stood in front of a fire and melted.

Why are goalkeepers always at the bank?
Because they're good savers.

Did you hear about the undertaker who buried a person in the wrong place?
It was a grave error.

Optician: Have your eyes ever been checked?
Customer: No, always plain blue.

I'm learning to be a barber.

Is it taking long?

No, I'm studying all the short cuts.

Barber: How would you like your hair cut?
Customer: Shorter, please.

What did the actor say when the trapdoor opened?
Don't worry, it's just a stage I'm going through.

If athletes get athlete's foot, what do rocket scientists get?
Missile-toe.

Waiter, waiter!

Waiter, I can't eat this disgusting food.
Get the manager.
It's no use, ma'am, he won't eat it either.

Waiter, waiter! My water's cloudy.
You're mistaken, ma'am. That's the dirt on the glass.

Waiter, this cheese is full of holes.
It could be worse, sir. It used to be full of maggots.

Cops and robbers

What does a policeman use to tell you the time?
A crime watch.

What happened to the burglar who broke into a calendar factory?
He got twelve months.

What happened to the burglar who fell into a cement mixer?
He became a hardened criminal.

Why did the thief saw the legs off his bed?
He wanted to lie low.

Why was the photographer arrested?
The police found his prints at the scene of a crime.

Did you hear about the man who was arrested for selling self-portraits?
He was framed.

Why are police officers so strong?
Because they hold up traffic.

What happened to the robber who stole a lamp?
He got a light sentence.

Why do criminals shower so often?
They like to make a clean getaway.

Silly sports

Why are babies fast swimmers?
Because they're good at the crawl.

What do you call a bird at the end of
a marathon?
Puffin.

Why are baseball fields so valuable?
Because they have a diamond in the middle.

What country do jockeys come from?
Horse-tralia.

What drink do soccer players like least?
Penal-tea.

Why didn't the two elephants enter
the swimming race?
**They only had one pair of trunks
between them.**

What drink do boxers like best?
Punch.

What happened to the soccer player whose eyesight began to fail?
He became a referee.

Doctor, doctor!

Doctor, doctor! Whenever I drink coffee, I get a terrible pain in my eye.
Hmm, try taking the spoon out of the cup.

Doctor, doctor, I feel like an ice cream cone.
Me too – I think I'll go out and buy one.

Doctor, doctor, will you take my temperature?
No need, I have one of my own.

Doctor, doctor, I feel like a clock.

You're too wound up.

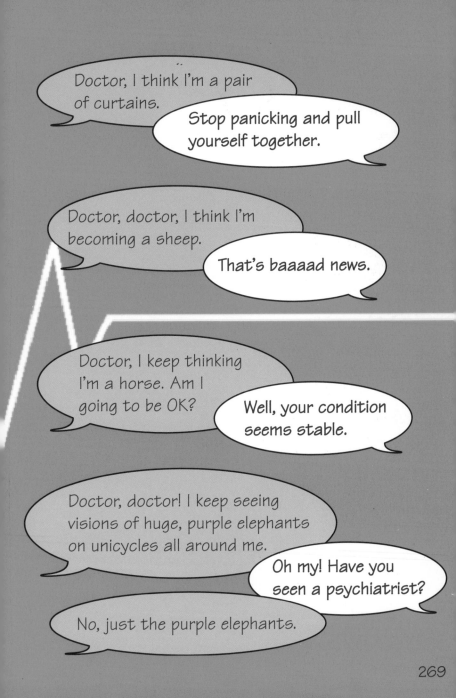

Shiver me timbers!

What do you call a pirate who
makes lots of mistakes?
Wrong John Silver.

Where do you take a sick pirate ship?
To the dock.

What toys do pirates' children like to play with?
Yo-ho-ho-yos.

How do you make a pirate angry?
Take away the "p" and he becomes irate.

Why couldn't the pirates play cards?
The captain was standing on the deck.

Why did the pirate have twigs in his beard?
He'd been sleeping in the crow's nest.

Everyday Laughs

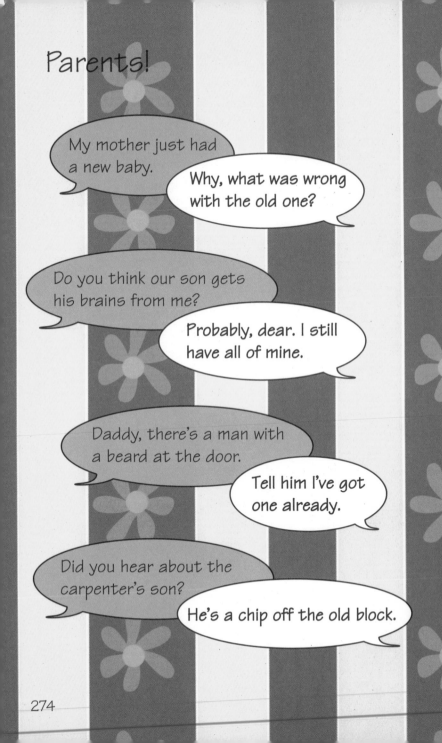

Silly siblings

Classroom capers

Hilarious holidays

A feast of fun

Why do lions eat raw meat?

Have you ever tried to teach one to cook?

Should you stir your coffee with your left hand or your right?

Neither, you should use a spoon.

Why did the tomato turn red?

Because it saw the salad dressing.

What did the hungry computer eat?

Chips, one byte at a time.

What's yellow and fills fields with music?

Pop-corn.

What did one plate say to the other?

Lunch is on me.

What's round, white and giggles?

A tickled onion.

What's worse than finding a maggot in your apple?

Finding half a maggot.

Getting around

What do you call a stupid boat?
An idi-yacht.

What did the traffic lights say to the traffic?
Don't peek, I'm changing.

What form of transport do carpenters prefer?
Planes!

What sport do flat fish like best?
Skate-boarding.

What happens to broken-down frogs?

They get toad away.

Worn-out jokes

What did the tie say to the hat?

You go on ahead while I hang around.

Did you hear about the boy who put on a clean pair of socks every day?

By the end of the week he couldn't get his shoes on.

How should you dress on a cold day?

Quickly.

What clothing can you make out of two banana skins?

A pair of slippers.

First published in 2003 by Usborne Publishing Ltd.,
Usborne House, 83-85 Saffron Hill, London, EC1N 8RT, England.
www.usborne.com

Copyright © 2003 Usborne Publishing Ltd.

The name Usborne and the devices ♀ ⊕ are
Trade Marks of Usborne Publishing Ltd.

...ed. No part of this publication may be reproduced,
...al system or transmitted in any form or by any
...chanical, photocopying, recording or otherwise,
...prior permission of the publisher.

...t published in America 2003
Printed in Italy